Introduction

Small ice cubes floating in a glass are a familiar sight to us all; we stir them with a straw to make our drink cooler. Who knows how many times we have done this without even thinking about it—a totally normal gesture. And yet it is precisely because of such an apparently banal fact as ice floating that the Earth has been able to develop and harbor life!

Instead of contracting when solidifying as all other substances do, water increases in volume and, naturally, floats.

Let's try to imagine what would happen if the ice were to go to the bottom. It would slowly fill up an alpine lake, for example, until it became a huge and totally solid mass, and the same process would occur in the oceans of the polar zones, which would end up totally lacking in life. Fortunately, this is not the case, but perhaps now we will look at our ice cubes with different eyes.

Water has many other unique properties. For example, it transmits heat better than any other liquid, which makes it possible for oceans to absorb heat in warm periods and then release it in cold periods, as if the seas were large rechargeable thermal batteries that attenuate the seasonal changes in the temperature of the atmosphere.

Furthermore, water can dissolve an incredible number of substances, so much so that it could be called the "universal solvent." During their long course, rivers absorb minerals and salts and transport them to the sea, thus determining their composition. The water in the primordial seas was much different, and millions of years ago, it was less salty than the seas we swim in during our vacations.

Three-quarters of the planet we call Earth are covered with water. And even about 70% of our bodies consist of water. But where does all this water come from?

• Nusa Penida, Indonesia

There are several different theories regarding the origin of the seas. Some say that the formation came about through complex chemical-physical processes; other "simpler" hypotheses affirm that water was the result of the impact of millions of comets, which consist mostly of ice, therefore suggesting that water came from outer space.

But we need not delve into this subject. We need only know that the Earth was in the right place at the right time. Had it been a little closer or a little further distant from the Sun, the temperatures that make life possible would not have existed. A few hundred million years too early, or millions of years too late (mere instants in the scale of cosmic time), and we would not be here to discuss this subject.

Sunlight penetrates the sea for only a few feet, but this is enough to make microscopic unicellular algae flourish. This algae, almost invisible, makes up the largest biomass on our planet and provides oxygen not only for water but also for the atmosphere. Indeed, most of the oxygen in the air that we breathe comes from the sea! Were we to ideally cover the surface of the sea with a sheet of plastic, all life would die of suffocation. A very disturbing thought, without a doubt, which should make us reflect and reconsider "the preservation of the sea" as a merely fashionable expression.

Therefore, the sea is, in the literal sense of the word, the largest reservoir of life on Earth. It is certainly the largest, monstrously so for humans, but it is not infinite, and while it has taken rivers millions of years to salt the sea and nourish it, human activity can destroy it in a much much shorter time. Proof of this is so evident that sophisticated instruments are not necessary to verify it. We need only put on a diving mask and observe the stretches of dead coral on a reef of the Maldive Islands, or see the disgusting spectacle of oil slicks drifting for thousands of miles and then washing up on the sand of our beaches.

When we dip our feet into the water at the seaside, what we are actually doing is putting them in all seas, for the simple reason that they are all connected. It therefore becomes immediately apparent that a pollutant in one sea will soon spread to all the seas in the world. The problems created in one country do not concern only its inhabitants, but the fauna, flora, and population of the entire globe.

A coastline beaten by the waves is no less fascinating than a white tropical beach with warm and transparent water. The protagonist is always the sea, an "actor" who knows how to interpret the most tender and romantic roles as convincingly as those of a violent and cruel subject.

In the following pages, through an extraordinary series of spectacular images, you will be able to admire the beauty of the various aspects of the sea, when it is calm and inviting and when it is frightening and the waves seem to be able to sweep away all obstacles, in a relentless and destructive outburst.

Ever since the most distant past the sea has fascinated humans, precisely because of its capricious nature, which has marked the history of navigation, a constant challenge for sailors: when the sea was calm the sails of the vessels would dangle immobile while waiting for the wind, while a sudden storm could toss even a large oil tanker around like a walnut shell.

Our modern ships are the fruit of the experience of the great navigators and of technology, and they now sail safely in any sea. But has this technological progress gone hand in hand with respect for the seas we have sailed? While this was not the case in the past, it is imperative that it be done now and in the future. The images in this book, which illustrate both the gelid water of the two poles and the coral reefs in the tropics, are not and must not become a mere historic document, but the testimony of how the sea must be preserved for us and for future generations.

THE SEA

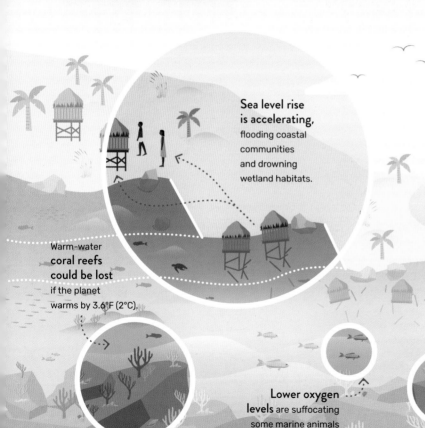

Sea level rise
is accelerating,
flooding coastal
communities
and drowning
wetland habitats.

Warm-water
**coral reefs
could be lost**
if the planet
warms by 3.6°F (2°C).

**Lower oxygen
levels** are suffocating
some marine animals
and shrinking their habitats.

At least
8.8 million tons
(8 million metric tons)
of plastic end up in our
oceans every year.

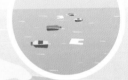

**More acidic
water** harms
animals that build
shells, such as corals,
clams, and oysters.

Larger and more frequent **blooms of toxic algae** are making fish, birds, marine mammals, and people sick.

The ocean absorbs **90%** of excess heat but at the cost of causing significant harm to marine ecosystems.

The ocean absorbs **30%** of CO_2

Disruptions in fisheries affect the marine food web, local livelihoods, and global food security.

37% of marine mammals are currently considered **endangered**.

Sources: Intergovernmental Panel on Climate Change, National Oceanic and Atmospheric Administration

The Coasts

Without water, our planet would be
one of the billions of lifeless rocks
floating endlessly in the vastness of
the inky-black void.

| *Fabien Cousteau*

The sea is a great sculptor: wherever it touches land, it shapes and molds it, consumes it, or covers it with sand, forming beaches, creating or eliminating entire islands.

The level of the sea has changed over the millennia, becoming lower during the glacial eras and rising in the interglacial periods. If we could observe a map of Earth during the last glaciation, which ended about 12,000 years ago, we would not be able to recognize the profile of the continents as they appear today on a globe. One of the greatest worries we have at present is the rise of the sea level caused by the melting of the polar ice because of global warming, a phenomenon that is unfortunately determined mostly by human activity, which implies very little time compared to natural processes, which take place over periods of thousands or even millions of years.

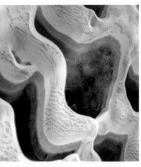

This problem immediately brings to mind, as usual, matters that concern us directly: houses flooded, wildfires, impassable roads, works of art destroyed, etc. But these are only the most evident effects of this type of circumstances, because the coasts are a particular habitat for plants and animals that have adapted to them after millions of years of evolution and that might not be able to tolerate such a rapid and drastic upheaval, which would trigger a series of disastrous consequences for the entire marine and terrestrial ecosystems.

The rocky coasts are those with the most biodiversity, and those who love snorkeling know quite well that if they want to admire the marine fauna they must swim among cliffs and underwater rocks, where animal life is abundant and varied, while they will see very little on the sand. The surface itself of the rocks is completely covered with a layer of animal and plant organisms, which in turn attract a multitude of fish and other animals, creating an environment that is particularly rich and ecologically important.

Unfortunately, we must admit that it is these very coastlines that in many countries have been literally invaded by constructions linked to tourism, so much so that the natural environment has disappeared under a continuous layer of houses and hotels.

While this may have been justified 100 years ago either due to ignorance or to the vital need of the fishermen's communities, nowadays it is no longer tolerable and, despite the fact that the data at our disposal would be enough to convince people to bring this destructive behavior to a halt, we still continue to build along the seashore with impunity, albeit in a slightly more controlled manner.

We are all familiar with the phenomenon of sea tides, which is caused principally by the gravitational pull of the Moon: twice a day the sea level rises during high tide and lowers during low tide. This difference in level is not equal along all the coasts. For example, in the Mediterranean, on beaches that descend slightly toward the sea, the water recedes for a few meters and then covers the sand during high tide. On the other hand, along the rocky coasts there is a very visible stripe of color that runs along the rocks and cliffs, marking the maximum height of the water during high tide. And in some oceanic coasts, the tides may reach a difference in level of more than 33 feet (10 m).

Thus, even when it is calm the sea is in continuous movement. And if we stop to think of the billions of square feet of water involved in this movement—even near the coasts where the quantity is at a minimum—it is easy to imagine the energy created by this natural phenomenon.

In fact, someone has thought about this and in some areas there are generators at work exploiting the to and fro of the sea. The principle is quite similar to that of wind turbines, although the system obviously differs: special turbines rotate in one direction when the sea is receding and in the opposite direction during high tide, thus exploiting the energy, known as "tidal power," of both movements—a technological procedure that might have interesting developments, since it makes use of an alternative and sustainable source of energy.

However, the sea is not always friendly and may very well become a destructive force through storms causing tidal surges, or even tsunamis created by underwater earthquakes or volcanic eruptions that sweep over the coasts for miles and miles.

In any case, these are natural events that have been occurring since the beginning of time and that also serve to revive marine life. On the contrary, the damage caused by human activity never stops. It does not grant respite and the natural environment hasn't got the time to recover.

The coasts are our natural contact with the sea, and respecting their environment is the first step toward being able to observe the sea as far as the horizon without feeling guilty about the tragic mistakes we have made and with the commitment to avoid making other such mistakes.

THE COASTS

Several countries could face extensive sandy beach erosion issues by the end of the 21st century, affecting about 50% of their sandy coastline.

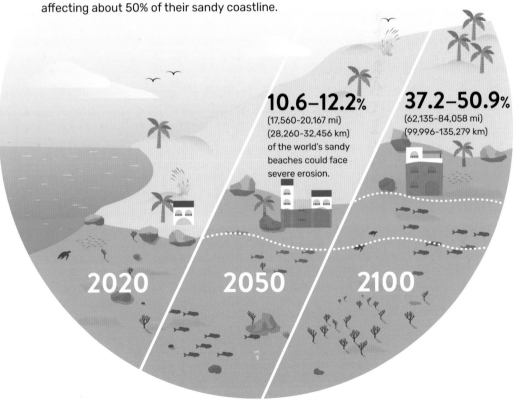

10.6–12.2%
(17,560-20,167 mi)
(28,260-32,456 km)
of the world's sandy beaches could face severe erosion.

37.2–50.9%
(62,135-84,058 mi)
(99,996-135,279 km)

2020

2050

2100

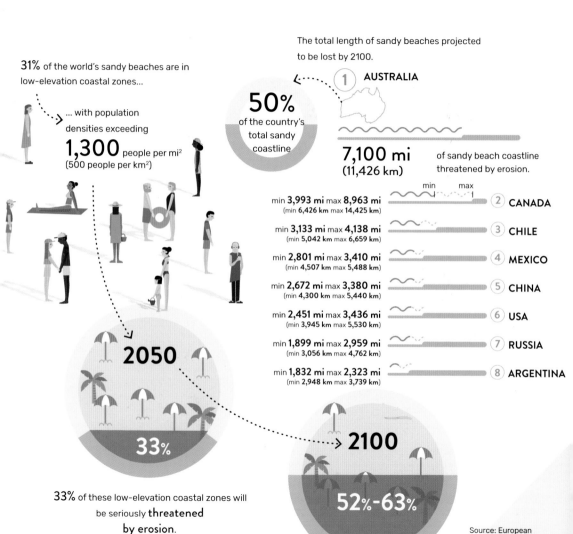

31% of the world's sandy beaches are in low-elevation coastal zones...

... with population densities exceeding **1,300** people per mi² (500 people per km²)

The total length of sandy beaches projected to be lost by 2100.

50% of the country's total sandy coastline

1 **AUSTRALIA**

7,100 mi (11,426 km) of sandy beach coastline threatened by erosion.

min **3,993 mi** max **8,963 mi** (min 6,426 km max 14,425 km) **2** **CANADA**

min **3,133 mi** max **4,138 mi** (min 5,042 km max 6,659 km) **3** **CHILE**

min **2,801 mi** max **3,410 mi** (min 4,507 km max 5,488 km) **4** **MEXICO**

min **2,672 mi** max **3,380 mi** (min 4,300 km max 5,440 km) **5** **CHINA**

min **2,451 mi** max **3,436 mi** (min 3,945 km max 5,530 km) **6** **USA**

min **1,899 mi** max **2,959 mi** (min 3,056 km max 4,762 km) **7** **RUSSIA**

min **1,832 mi** max **2,323 mi** (min 2,948 km max 3,739 km) **8** **ARGENTINA**

2050

33%

2100

52%-63%

33% of these low-elevation coastal zones will be seriously **threatened by erosion**.

Source: European Commission's Joint Research Centre (JRC)

Sunnylvsfjorden, Norway

No water, no life. No blue, no green.
It is the worst of times but it is the best
of times because we still have a chance.
Many of us ask what can I, as one
person, do, but history shows us that
everything good and bad starts because
somebody does something or does not
do something.

| *Sylvia Earle*

The sea does not reward those who
are too anxious, too greedy, or too
impatient. Patience, patience, patience,
is what the sea teaches. Patience
and faith. One should lie empty, open,
choiceless as a beach—waiting for
a gift from the sea.

| *Anne Morrow Lindbergh*

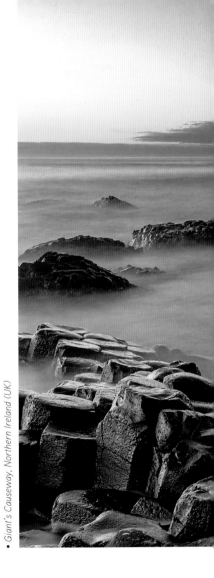

• *Giant's Causeway, Northern Ireland (UK)*

There's nothing more beautiful than the way the ocean refuses to stop kissing the shoreline, no matter how many times it's sent away.

| *Sarah Kay*

• *Seven Sisters cliffs, England (UK)*

All the king's horses and all the king's men will never gather up all the plastic and put the ocean back together again. Only we humans make waste that nature can't digest.

| *Charles Moore*

We're plundering the ocean and its vital resources, and just because we can't see the devastation from dry land doesn't mean it's any less dangerous. It needs to stop.

| *Leonardo DiCaprio*

Nature doesn't need people—people need nature; nature would survive the extinction of the human being and go on just fine, but human culture, human beings, cannot survive without nature.

| *Harrison Ford*

Calanque de Morgiou, Provence, France

Every time I stand before a beautiful beach, its waves seem to whisper to me:
If you choose the simple things and find joy in nature's simple treasures, life
and living need not be so hard.

| *Psyche Roxas-Mendoza*

32 • Darss Peninsula, Germany 33 • Møn Island, Denmark

• Capo Vaticano, Calabria, Italy

Understanding the importance of
the beach's role vis-a-vis the land,
the nearshore, and the ocean and its
biodiversity is crucial to its protection
and preservation.

| *Orrin H. Pilkey*

Why do we think of the ocean as a mere storehouse of food, oil, and minerals? The sea is not a bargain basement. The greatest resource of the ocean is not material but the boundless spring of inspiration and well-being we gain from her. Yet we risk poisoning the sea forever just when we are learning her science, art, and philosophy and how to live in her embrace.

| *Jacques-Yves Cousteau*

• Eastern Sinai Peninsula, Egypt 42–43 • Skeleton Coast, Namibia 44–45 • Table Mountain, Western Cape, South Africa

At the beach, life is different. Time doesn't move hour to hour but mood to moment. We live by the currents, plan with the tides and follow the sun.

| *Sandy Gingras*

When anxious, uneasy and bad thoughts
come, I go to the sea, and the sea
drowns them out with its great wide
sounds, cleanses me with its noise, and
imposes a rhythm upon everything in me
that is bewildered and confused.

| *Rainer Maria Rilke*

• *Mughsail Beach, Oman*

• *Tangalle Beach, Sri Lanka*

There is no question that the beaches that our grandchildren will play on will be different from ours. The important question is whether they will be better or worse.

| *Orrin H. Pilkey*

We not only need a rapid transition to a low-carbon economy that prevents the most cataclysmic consequences of global warming, we need real dollars and real planning for coastal protection to combat the consequences that are already inevitable.

| *Bill de Blasio*

• *The Twelve Apostles, Victoria, Australia*

And it is an interesting biological fact
that all of us have, in our veins the exact
same percentage of salt in our blood
that exists in the ocean, and, therefore,
we have salt in our blood, in our sweat,
in our tears. We are tied to the ocean.
And when we go back to the sea, we are
going back from whence we came.

| *John F. Kennedy*

Emissions of greenhouse gases
warm the planet, altering the carbon
and water cycles. A warmer ocean
stores more heat, providing more fuel
for hurricanes. A warmer atmosphere
holds more water, bringing dangerous
deluges. Rising sea levels threaten
coastal zones.

| *Johan Rockström*

• *Whitehaven Beach, Queensland, Australia*

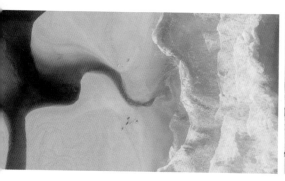

A beach is not only a sweep of sand,
but shells of sea creatures, the sea
glass, the seaweed, the incongruous
objects washed up by the ocean.

| *Henry Grunwald*

56 left • *Yeagarup Beach, Western Australia, Australia* 56 right • *Lucky Bay, Western Australia, Australia*
57 • *Two People Bay, Western Australia, Australia*

• Cathedral Cove, New Zealand 60–61 • Gulf of St. Lawrence, Canada

Our oceans are on the verge of collapse and we have all played a huge role in this. Now we must all play our part to stop it. Without oceans, the Earth would simply not function.

| *Javier Bardem*

Acadia National Park, Maine (USA)

Even if you never have the chance to see or touch the ocean, it touches you with every breath you take, every drop of water you drink, every bite you consume. Everyone, everywhere is inextricably connected to and utterly dependent upon the existence of the sea.

| *Sylvia Earle*

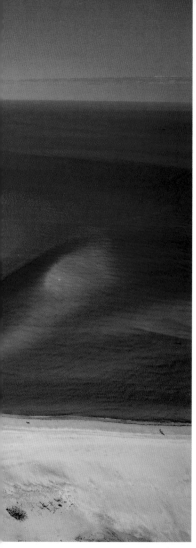

• Caladesi Island State Park, Florida (USA)

The ocean is the lifeblood of our world. If we were to lose our fish that we appreciate so much by overfishing; or if we were to lose some of our favorite beaches to overbuilding and pollution, then how would we feel? It's become a case of not knowing what you've got until it's gone.

| *Aaron Peirsol*

The beach to me is a sacred zone between the Earth and the sea, one of those in-between between places where transitions can be experienced—where endings can be mourned and beginnings birthed. A walk along the beach offers the gift of the unexpected.

| *Joan Anderson*

• Bandon Beach, Oregon (USA) 68–69 • Oregon Coast (USA)
70-71 • Ecola State Park, Oregon (USA) 72-73 • Cabo San Lucas, Baja California, Mexico

This is the moment when we must
come together to save this planet.
Let us resolve that we will not leave our
children a world where the oceans rise
and famine spreads and terrible storms
devastate our lands.

| *Barack Obama*

• Mobula ray, Sea of Cortez, Mexico

To me, the sea is like a person—like a child that I've known a long time. It sounds crazy, I know, but when I swim in the sea I talk to it. I never feel alone when I'm out there.

| Gertrude Ederle

You go to a beach, you see a lot of plastic. It's out of the ocean, it stays out of the ocean, so that's good. But the thing is that in this Great Pacific garbage patch, this area twice the size of Texas, there's no coastlines to collect plastic.

| *Boyan Slat*

78-79 • Playa Cabuyal, Costa Rica 79 • Playa Carrillo, Costa Rica

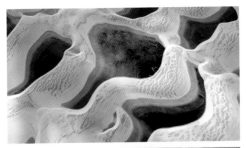

The Earth, the air, the land, and the
water are not an inheritance from
our forefathers but on loan from
our children. So we have to hand over
to them at least as it was handed
over to us.

| *Gandhi*

• *Lençóis Maranhenses National Park, Brazil*

• Beach of Morro Branco, Brazil

The sea is everything. It covers seven
tenths of the terrestrial globe. Its breath
is pure and healthy. It is an immense
desert, where man is never lonely,
for he feels life stirring on all sides.

| *Jules Verne*

• Beberibe Cliffs, Brazil

The ocean is being threatened from
multiple angles—it's a combination
of warming waters, overfishing,
and pollution, of which one is plastic.
We're putting stuff in that doesn't belong
there. We're taking stuff out that
does belong there.

| *Boyan Slat*

• *Paracas National Reserve, Peru*

The ocean gives us joy. The ocean gives
us oxygen. The ocean gives us food.
We give it plastic; we saturate it with
carbon; we pollute it and destroy it.
We must not allow what we will leave
to future generations to be the tragic
decline of our oceans and our unjustified
guilt for having favored their demise.

| *Richard Branson*

• La Portada de Antofagasta, Chile

The shore is an ancient world, for as long
as there has been an Earth and sea there
has been this place of the meeting of land
and water. Yet it is a world that keeps
alive the sense of continuing creation and
of the relentless drive of life.

| *Rachel Carson*

The Lords of the Sea

We have an obligation to fight for life on
Earth—not just for ourselves but for all those,
humans and others, who came before us and
to whom we are beholden, and for all those
who, if we are wise enough, will come after.

| *Carl Sagan*

One could say that water annuls the force of gravity and that this has made it possible for gigantic forms of life to evolve in the sea, precisely because they are not limited by their weight. So, are these creatures the true lords of the sea? If we ask this question of a naturalist, or better, a marine biologist, we would risk getting a rather complicated answer. For that matter, it is by no means easy to make a ranking of which animals dominate the seas more than others.

The huge blue whale, which is more than 98 feet (30 meters) long, has no rivals when it comes to size, and obviously it is placed at the top of our "ranking," since it is the largest animal that has ever lived on Earth. It swims in all the oceans, from the poles to the equator, and is perfectly at ease in its environment. But it has a problem: the most aggressive predator on Earth—man.

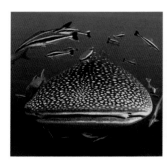

"There it blows!" was the shout whalers made when they sighted a large cetacean they would hunt for its meat, fat, oil, and from its fins, the famous whalebones used to make corsets for high society ladies. There was no hope for this large leviathan.

If we take a look at a book published only 60 years ago, we will be amazed to see that most of the photographs portray large cetaceans such as sperm whales that have been killed and are either tied to the sides of whalers or beached. Certainly, at that time we didn't have the technology that now allows us to take splendid photographs of these animals in their environment, depicting the characteristic behavior of their extraordinary lifestyle. While admiring them in this book, we can think that at this very moment, a sperm whale weighing 50 tons is diving to a depth of more than 6,561 feet (2,000 meters) in search of food.

Unfortunately, the lords of the sea have always attracted the avid attention of humans, and only in recent decades has this attention been transformed into admiration, respect, and awareness of the role these creatures play in the complex marine ecosystem. International agreements (which certain nations have refused to sign) have abolished hunting cetaceans and all those dominant species that have been transformed into prey and have almost disappeared from the oceans in which they have lived in perfect equilibrium for thousands of years.

Thanks to the measures taken to safeguard these extraordinary giants of the sea, their populations have been given a new lease on life. But in the case of certain species, the situation remains extremely critical, most of all because of the nations that have continued to hunt them.

Whale watching, going on a boat to observe large cetaceans from close up, is now a very widespread activity, and the enthusiasm of those who have the fortune to be the first to sight the spectacular breathing of a whale is not inferior to that of the whalers of the past, even though the objectives are quite different, fortunately.

The ocean is an extremely competitive environment, and at first sight, it might seem that it is nothing less than an arena, where predators and prey carry on their incessant struggle for survival. The proverb "big fish eats small fish," which also includes cetaceans, has some truth to it, but only up to a certain point.

It is also true that the oceans are the home to the largest predators on our planet, such as the great white shark, which can be as much as 19.7 feet (6 meters) long, and the killer whale, which, at more than 26 feet (8 meters) long, is the largest of all. However, there are also the peaceful "vegetarians" that feed on plankton: these include the whale shark, which, at 59 feet (18 meters) long and boasting elegant light blue skin with regular patterns of regular white stripes and dots, is a true lord of the sea.

The manta ray is quite a different matter. Similar to an enormous underwater bird, with a "wingspan" of almost 23 feet (7 meters), it filters plankton, ingesting large quantities with its large mouth.

All these astonishing creatures would seem to be able to dominate the seas without any danger. But their impressive size does not protect them from all the environmental alterations that are threatening the marine ecosystem. On the contrary, they often suffer from them more than other species because their food chains are more easily broken.

However, the true lords of the sea do not consist only of these spectacular giants but also include fish, which, more often than not, do not surprise us with their shape, beauty, or size, but with how they flourish, with enormous populations whose numbers are truly staggering. An example is the Atlantic cod, which once dominated the northern Atlantic with schools consisting of millions of individuals. Indiscriminate and massive fishing has practically exterminated this species, which at present is considered vulnerable. In those regions where this cod is still fished despite everything, there are no vigorous adults up to 5 feet (1.5 meters) long, but only young a few centimeters in length. Only the total suspension of Atlantic cod fishing may, perhaps, restore it to its former glory.

THE LORDS OF THE SEA

The decline of global whale population in pre-whaling periods versus the year 2001.

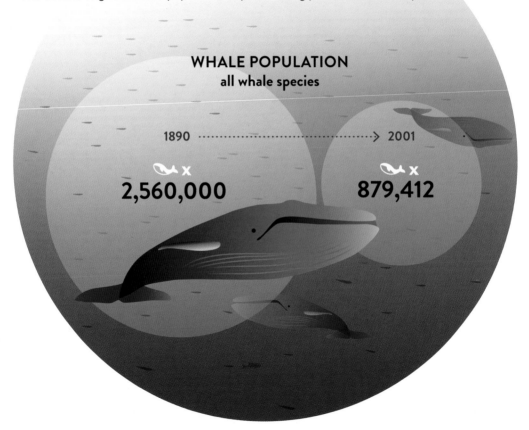

WHALE POPULATION
all whale species

1890 ···> 2001

🐋 x
2,560,000

🐋 x
879,412

Sea surface temperatures increased during the 20th century and continue to rise. From 1901 through 2020, **temperatures rose at an average rate of .14°F (.08°C) per decade.** In 2020, global ocean surface temperatures were 1.35°F (.75°C) higher than the 20th century average.

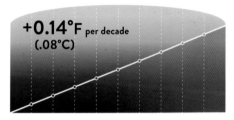

+0.14°F per decade
(.08°C)

1900 1910 1920 1930 1940 1950 1960 1970 1980 1990 2020

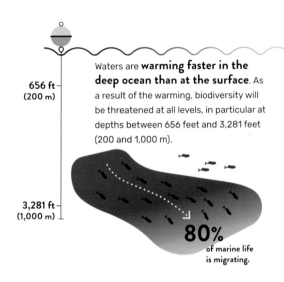

Waters are **warming faster in the deep ocean than at the surface.** As a result of the warming, biodiversity will be threatened at all levels, in particular at depths between 656 feet and 3,281 feet (200 and 1,000 m).

656 ft
(200 m)

3,281 ft
(1,000 m)

80%
of marine life
is migrating.

Ocean creatures rely on oxygen dissolved in seawater, but **climate change is gradually draining oxygen from the seas:** about 1–2% is thought to have been lost from 1960 to 2010, and that could rise to **4%** by 2100.

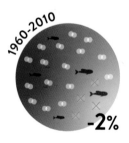

1960-2010

-2%

2100

-4%

In severe cases, **dissolved oxygen levels can fall so low that parts of the deep ocean become barren.**
A 2008 global survey found at least 405 of these dead zones, up from 49 in the 1960s.

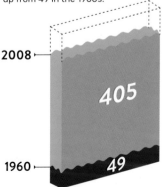

2008

405

1960

49

Sources: United States Environmental Protection Agency, The Ocean Foundation, Nature Climate Change, National Oceanic and Atmospheric Administration, China Dialogue Ocean

No aquarium, no tank in a marine land,
however spacious it may be, can begin
to duplicate the conditions of the sea.
And no dolphin who inhabits one of
those aquariums or one of those marine
lands can be considered normal.

| *Jacques-Yves Cousteau*

• Humpback whales

I am concerned about the air we breathe and the water we drink. If overfishing continues, if pollution continues, many of these species will disappear off the face of the Earth.

| Bernard Marcus

The industrial way we fish for seafood is harming the marine habitats that all ocean life depends upon. Indiscriminate commercial fishing practices that include miles of driftnets, long lines with thousands of lethal hooks and bottom trawls are ruining ocean ecosystems by killing non-seafood species, including sea turtles and marine mammals.

| *Ted Danson*

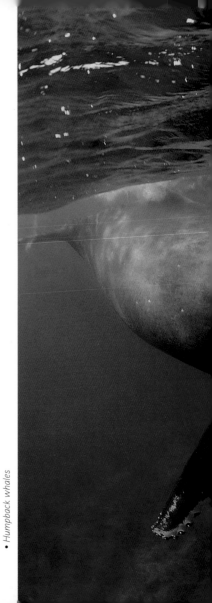

• Humpback whales

We owe it to our children to be better stewards of the environment. The alternative?—a world without whales. It's too terrible to imagine.

| *Pierce Brosnan*

We all know that most of the Earth
is covered with water, but typically
we see only the top of it. Beneath its
shimmering surface there is a world of
life, more intricately woven than that of
any rain forest.

| *Richard Ellis*

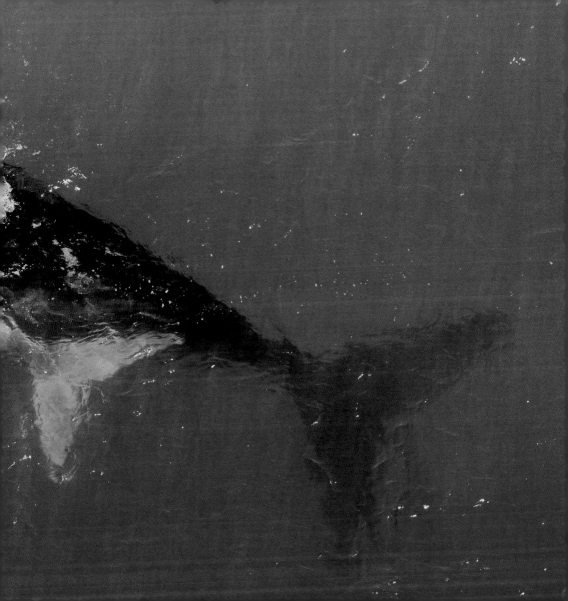

There is the life of the plankton in almost endless variety; there are the many kinds of fish, both surface and bottom living; there are the hosts of different invertebrate creatures on the sea-floor; and there are those almost grotesque forms of pelagic life in the oceans depths. Then there are the squids and cuttlefish, and the porpoises, dolphins and great whales.

| *Alister Hardy*

114-115 and 116-117 • Killer whales 118-119 • Whale shark

With over 50% of ocean surfaces being targeted by industrial fishing fleets, 90% of the large fish in the oceans, including tuna and sharks, have now vanished. We've eaten them in the last 100 years.

| *Enric Sala*

It is, surely, our responsibility to do everything within our power to create a planet that provides a home not just for us, but for all life on Earth.

| *Sir David Attenborough*

• *Giant manta rays*

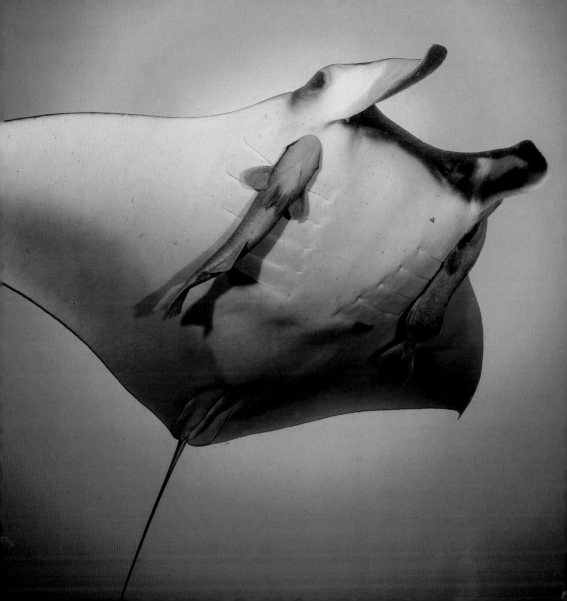

• Sand tiger shark

We provoke a shark every time we enter
the water where sharks happen to be,
for we forget: The ocean is not our
territory—it's theirs.

| *Peter Benchley*

• Sand tiger shark 134–135 • Shortfin mako shark

Sharks are beautiful animals, and if you're lucky enough to see lots of them, that means that you're in a healthy ocean. You should be afraid if you are in the ocean and don't see sharks.

| *Sylvia Earle*

136 • Lemon shark 137 left • Tiger shark and lemon shark 137 right • Caribbean reef sharks 138–139 and 140–141 • Great white sharks

The Islands

We are all surrounded by the ocean, even if we sometimes feel far away from it. Maybe that is why the many threats facing our oceans feel so distant from our hearts.

| *Javier Bardem*

What is an island? This is a question that is easily answered by taking a definition from the dictionary: a piece of land surrounded by water. If we stop to think that continents are completely surrounded by the sea, well, then they could also be considered islands. In truth, there is no precise way to define an island except, perhaps, by its size. For example, Australia, even though it is often called "the big island," is actually considered a subcontinent of Oceania. By convention, Greenland, which is about seven times larger than Italy, is considered the largest true island.

Deciding which is the smallest is even more difficult: among the innumerable islands in the coral atolls, many seem similar to those in classic cartoons, little piles of sand with or without a palm tree in the middle.

On top of that, these pearls in the ocean are subject to continuous changes and may even disappear after a storm with heavy seas.

In any case, the characteristic feature of an island is that its territory is surrounded and ends suddenly at the seaside. This may seem to be a banal consideration, but what is not banal is the fact that it has limited resources and they cannot be used without carefully taking their sustainability into account. A famous and sad example of this is Easter Island, which was exploited in the past by the natives in a totally irresponsible manner, becoming the island we see today: a desolate piece of land with monolithic heads that are not looking at the sea surrounding them, but rather gazing with melancholy at what was once a land covered with forests.

When landing on an island we do not realize we are standing on the top of a mountain whose slopes descend to the sea bottom. The most extraordinary islands are the oceanic ones. If we were able to observe them by ideally eliminating the water, we would see very tall pinnacles rising from the bottom of the ocean, emerging from the surface with their peaks. The base of the island of Hawaii, the largest in the archipelago of the same name, also known as the Big Island, lies at a depth of more than 31,824 feet (9,700 meters), almost 3,281 feet (1,000 meters) more than Mt. Everest.

Islands like these are created by the lava that erupts from underwater volcanoes; once it touches water, it solidifies almost instantly and accumulates, layer upon layer, until it reaches the surface of the ocean. All this usually takes thousands of years, but in the Hawaiian Islands, whose volcanoes are still active, there occurs something that is the opposite to the erosion that coasts usually experience. The lava that flows from the Kilauea volcano, which erupts continuously, reaches the ocean, and once cooled it forms new land, increasing the size of the Big Island, which from 1983 to 2002 has grown by more than 0.7 square miles (2 square km).

Not all islands are of volcanic origin; many are formed by breaking off from dry land through erosion, and others by the slow movements of the Earth's crust that have separated them from the continents. And recently another type of island has appeared, which represents in dramatic fashion the effects of present-day everyday life.

In fact, one often hears about "floating islands of garbage" as large as entire countries. Where and how do they originate?

Along the coasts of many countries there are dumps that continue to grow so much that they often extend into the sea. They could be called "peninsulas of refuse" and they consist almost entirely of plastic. This material "behaves" in a much more treacherous and noxious way than its disgusting aspect would intimate: under the power of the breakers, the various types of plastic disintegrate into tiny particles that range from a few millimeters to microscopic dimensions. But this certainly does not alter their attributes and nature as plastic! These pieces of "microplastic" are carried by the ocean currents and, as occurs, for example, in the case of the algae that form the Sargasso Sea, they are concentrated in vast areas of the oceans. This then creates immense "islands of garbage" that are practically invisible, which makes them all the more dangerous. In some areas there have even been concentrations of microplastic several times larger than the masses of zooplankton. The microplastic has wormed its way, so to speak, into the marine food chains, and it is certainly neither edible nor innocuous—quite the contrary. The effects it has, whether long-term or short-term, are rather unpredictable, but it has already been found in the fish that we eat.

Someone is developing systems in an attempt to stem this problem and possibly solve it, but time is not on our side. These "islands" not only must not increase, they must be eliminated as soon as possible because tomorrow may be too late.

To conclude, if we stop to think about it, the Earth itself is an island—large compared to us, but still always limited. And the territory we can live in is also limited, as are the resources we can use, and the space that makes our planet an island is an impassable sea.

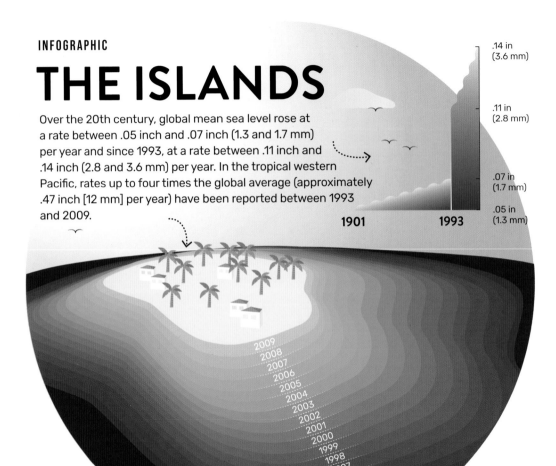

INFOGRAPHIC

THE ISLANDS

Over the 20th century, global mean sea level rose at a rate between .05 inch and .07 inch (1.3 and 1.7 mm) per year and since 1993, at a rate between .11 inch and .14 inch (2.8 and 3.6 mm) per year. In the tropical western Pacific, rates up to four times the global average (approximately .47 inch [12 mm] per year) have been reported between 1993 and 2009.

.14 in (3.6 mm)

.11 in (2.8 mm)

.07 in (1.7 mm)

.05 in (1.3 mm)

1901   1993

2009
2008
2007
2006
2005
2004
2003
2002
2001
2000
1999
1998
1997
1996
1995
1994
1993

(12 mm)

SOLOMON ISLANDS

5 islands have been **lost** due to sea-level rise and coastal erosion.

9 reef islands are severely eroded and likely to disappear.

Nuatambu Island, home to 25 families, has lost more than half of its habitable area, with **11 houses** washed into the sea.

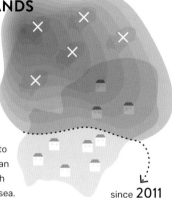

since **2011**

MALDIVES

As the flattest country on Earth, the **Republic of Maldives** is extremely vulnerable to rising sea levels.

Mid-level scenarios for global warming emissions

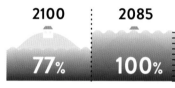

2100	2085
77%	**100%**
rise of **1.6 feet**/year (rise of .5 m/year)	rise of **3.3 feet**/year (rise of 1 m/year)

ATOLL OF TARAWA

The **Republic of Kiribati** is a low-lying Pacific island nation made up by an archipelago of 33 atolls—21 of them inhabited.

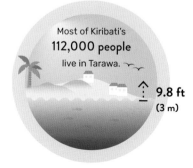

Most of Kiribati's **112,000 people** live in Tarawa.

The capital of Tarawa is **less than 9.8 feet (3 m)** above sea level.

↕ **9.8 ft (3 m)**

GREAT PACIFIC GARBAGE PATCH

1.8 trillion pieces of plastic weighing **88,185 tons** (80,000 metric tons).

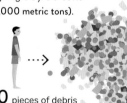

3x France

250 pieces of debris **for every human** in the world.

Sources: Environmental Research Letters, Intergovernmental Panel on Climate Change, Union of Concerned Scientists, The Ocean Cleanup

• Reynisfjara Beach, Iceland 152–153 • Vágar, Faroe Islands (Denmark)

We must address the climate crisis,
if we're going to address the ocean.
The number one issue with the ocean
is acidification and the number one
issue with acidification is carbon.
Number one, and first and foremost,
we must all become net-zero. Every
company, every country, every
organization, every individual must
commit now to becoming net-zero.

| *Marc Benioff*

• Neist Point, Isle of Skye, Scotland (UK)

It is a curious situation that the sea, from which life first arose, should now be threatened by the activities of one form of that life. But the sea, though changed in a sinister way, will continue to exist: the threat is rather to life itself.

| *Rachel Carson*

The high seas constitutes two-thirds of the oceans and covers nearly half the planet's surface, and harbors the largest remaining reservoir of unexplored biodiversity left on Earth. Yet these waters face escalating pressure from overfishing, deep seabed mining, ocean acidification, chemical and noise pollution, huge gyres of plastic waste, dead zones, ship traffic and destructive fishing tactics such as bottom trawling.

| *Richard Branson*

• Lofoten Islands, Norway

Our oceans feed us, protect us, regulate our climate, our weather, anchor industries from transportation to tourism to trade of all kind. The health of our planet's oceans determine in large part the health of our own bodies and the health of our economies.

| *Barack Obama*

• *Madeira, Portugal*

• Formentera, Balearic Islands, Spain

160

I hope for your help to explore and protect the wild ocean in ways that will restore the health and, in so doing, secure hope for humankind. Health to the ocean means health for us.

| *Sylvia Earle*

If you're overfishing at the top of the
food chain, and acidifying the ocean at
the bottom, you're creating a squeeze
that could conceivably collapse the
whole system.

| *Carl Safina*

162 top • Archipelago of Lavezzi, Corsica, France 162 bottom • Beach of Santa Giulia, Corsica, France

163 • Port de Girolata, Corsica, France

Ocean health is a moral imperative,
a business imperative and a matter
of global and national security. It should
be recognized as a vital building block
of peace and prosperity.

| *Queen Noor of Jordan*

Since oceans are the life support system of our planet, regulating the climate, providing most of our oxygen and feeding over a billion people, what's bad for oceans is bad for us—very bad.

| *Philippe Cousteau Jr.*

• Sinis Peninsula, Sardinia, Italy

We absolutely need to clean up the
plastic that's already in the ocean.
It won't go away by itself. But we do also
need to make sure that no more plastic
enters the oceans in the first place.
These things should go hand in hand.

| *Boyan Slat*

We're going to lose more species, acidify the oceans more, do damage that it will take millions of years—if not longer—to unwind. Exactly how much damage will we do? How deep will those scars run? We don't know yet. But we will turn the ship.

| *Ramez Naam*

• *Vulcano, Aeolian Islands, Sicily, Italy*

For most of history, man has had to fight
nature to survive; in this century he
is beginning to realize that, in order to
survive, he must protect it.

| *Jacques-Yves Cousteau*

174 • *Rabbit Island, Lampedusa, Italy*
175 • *Rabbit Beach, Lampedusa, Italy*

Ocean had given me hope. He'd made me believe in people again. His sincerity had rubbed me raw, had peeled back the stubborn layers of anger I'd lived in for so long. Ocean made me want to give the world a second chance.

| *Tahereh Mafi*

• *Azure Window, Gozo, Malta*

If we don't preserve the oceans from nitrate runoff and plastic and chemicals, and if we don't preserve it from acidification, and if we don't preserve it from grotesque overfishing, we're going to have the most massive ecosystem on the planet in peril.

| *John F. Kerry*

178-179 • *Island of Dugi Otok, Croatia*
179 • *Kornati archipelago, Croatia*

180-181 • Navagio Beach, Zante, Greece 181 top • Porto Katsiki, Lefkada, Greece
181 bottom • Canal D'amour Beach, Corfu, Greece

The sea possesses a power over one's
moods that has the effect of a will.
The sea can hypnotize. Nature in general
can do so.

| *Henrik Ibsen*

Waves are the voices of tides. Tides
are life. They bring new food for shore
creatures and take ships out to sea.
They are the ocean's pulse, and our own
heartbeat.

| *Tamora Pierce*

The ocean has always been a salve to my soul . . . The best thing for a cut or abrasion was to go swimming in salt water. Later down the road of life, I made the discovery that salt water was also good for the mental abrasions one inevitably acquires on land.

| *Jimmy Buffett*

• *Balos Lagoon, Crete, Greece*

Every fish you throw back into the ocean is a triumph of the idea that human beings can be better. I do my best, every day, to throw at least one fish back into the ocean. I hope that you will join me.

| *Olivia Atwater*

I believe in the ocean curing all bad moods. I believe in the waves wiping away worries. I believe in seashells bringing good luck. I believe in toes in the sand grounding my soul.

| *Unknown*

• *Los Hervideros, Lanzarote, Canary Islands, Spain*

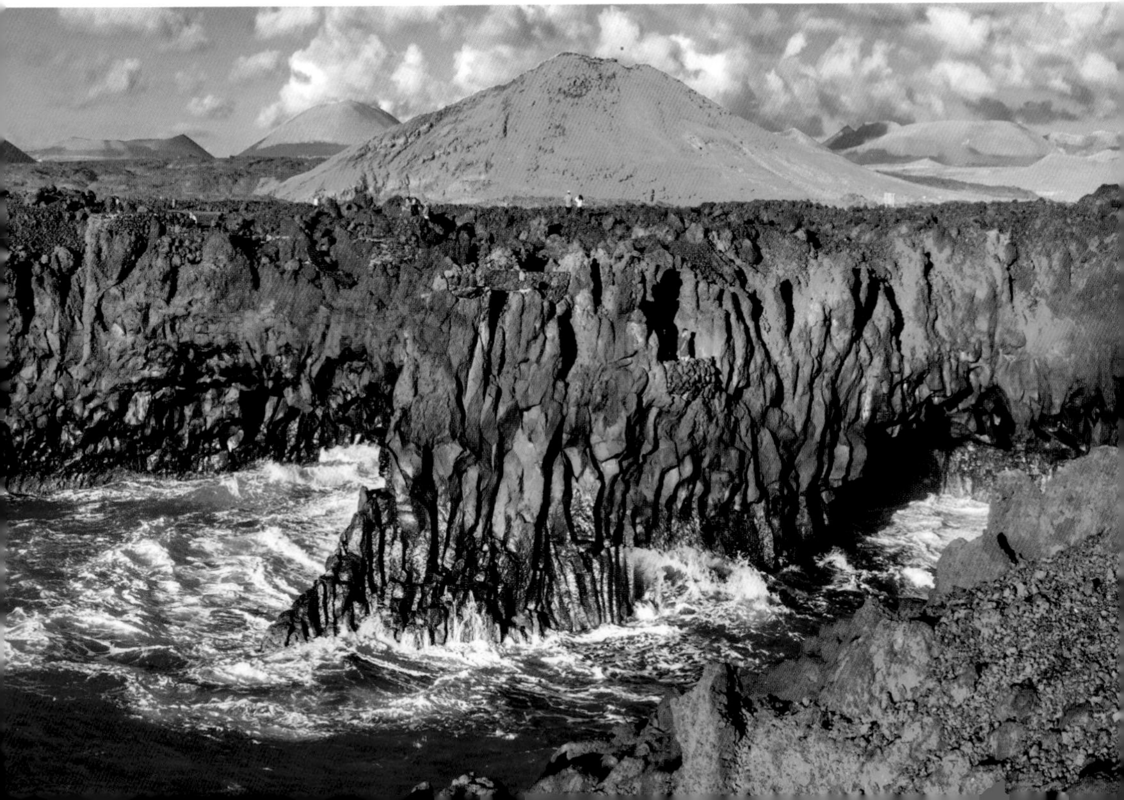

The strongest governments on Earth
cannot clean up pollution by themselves.
They must rely on each ordinary person,
like you and me, on our choices, and on
our will.

| *Chai Jing*

190 left • Desert rose, Socotra, Yemen 190 right and 191 • Socotra, Yemen
192–193 • La Digue Island, Seychelles

The beach is truly home, its broad
expanse of sand as welcoming as a
mother's open arms. What's more, this
landscape, which extends as far as the
eye can see, always reminds me of
possibility.

| *Joan Anderson*

194 left • Zanzibar, Tanzania 194 right • Pamunda Island, Zanzibar, Tanzania 195 • Zanzibar, Tanzania

Le Morne, Mauritius

I felt the full breadth and depth of the ocean around the sphere of the Earth, back billions of years to the beginning of life, across all the passing lives and deaths, the endless waves of swimming joy and quiet losses of exquisite creatures with fins and fronds, tentacles and wings, colorful and transparent, tiny and huge, coming and going. There is nothing the ocean has not seen.

| *Sally Andrew*

Stop eating the ocean. There is no such thing as a sustainable fishery. And be cognizant of the fact that if the oceans die, we die. Our ultimate responsibility is to protect biodiversity in our world's oceans.

| *Paul Watson*

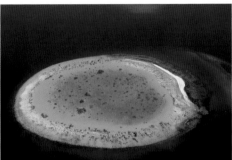

The oceans belong to us all, but
their fate is now in the hands of the
delegates. The instinct to protect
is one of humanity's noblest traits.
Please embody this principle.
Please protect our oceans.

| *Javier Bardem*

• *Maldives*

• Maldives

• Phang Nga Bay, Thailand

With every drop of water you drink,
every breath you take, you're connected
to the sea. No matter where on Earth
you live. Most of the oxygen in the
atmosphere is generated by the sea.

| *Sylvia Earle*

The ocean knows no borders—you don't have to use your passport—so we need to work along the lines of the natural marine ecosystems. Neighbouring countries must work together.

| *Isabella Lövin*

• *Ha Long Bay, Vietnam*

Coron Island, Philippines

• *Palawan, Philippines*

Don't you realize that the sea is the home of water? All water is off on a journey unless it's in the sea, and it's homesick, and bound to make its way home someday.

| *Zora Neale Hurston*

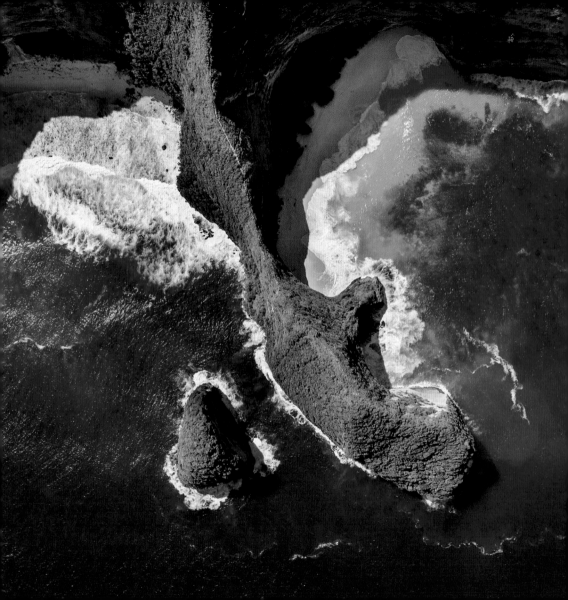

The three great elemental sounds in
nature are the sound of rain, the sound
of wind in a primeval wood, and the
sound of outer ocean on a beach.
I have heard them all, and of the three
elemental voices, that of ocean is the
most awesome, beautiful and varied.

| *Henry Beston*

• *Nusa Penida Island, Bali, Indonesia*

The sea enchants, the sea kills, it moves, it frightens, it also makes you laugh, at times, it disappears every now and then, it disguises itself as a lake, or it builds storms, it devours ships, it gives wealth away, it doesn't give any answers, it is wise, it is sweet, it is powerful, it is unpredictable. But above all: the sea calls.

| *Alessandro Baricco*

● *Miyakojima, Ryukyu Archipelago, Japan*

To survive today, other animals must endure global warming, pollution, and fewer habitats. More tragically, they must endure the silence of human hearts.

| *Anthony Douglas Williams*

The ocean makes me feel really small and it makes me put my whole life into perspective . . . It humbles you and makes you feel almost like you've been baptized. I feel born again when I get out of the ocean.

| *Beyoncé Knowles*

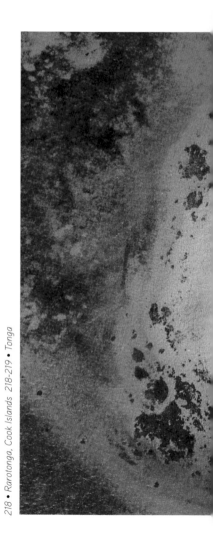

218 • Rarotonga, Cook Islands 218-219 • Tonga

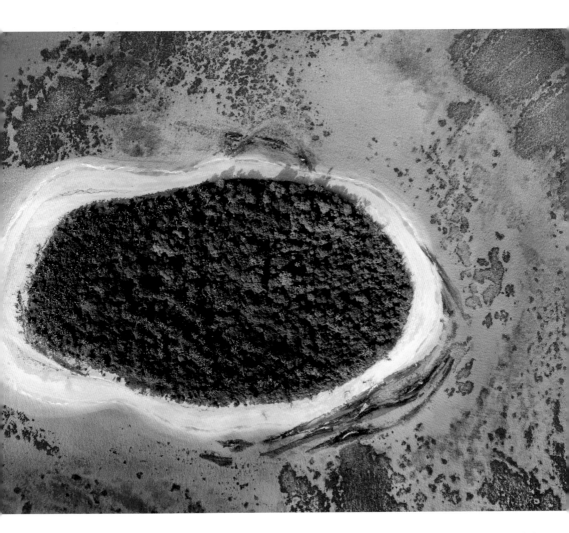

• Dravuni Island, Fiji

I often struggle to find words that will communicate the vastness of the Pacific Ocean to people who have never been to sea. Yet as I gazed from the deck at the surface of what ought to have been a pristine ocean, I was confronted, as far as the eye could see, with the sight of plastic.

| *Charles Moore*

• Rangiroa, French Polynesia

A healthy ocean is our most important
ally in fighting the effects of climate
change. We have the opportunity to act.
We know what the solutions may be.
Let's get to work!

| *Richard Branson*

• Bora Bora, French Polynesia 224–225 • Fatu Hiva, Marquesas Islands, French Polynesia

• *Na Pali Coast, Kauai, Hawaii (USA)*

In Hawaii we understand why
it is important to "malama," or to take
care of, our land, our oceans, and air—
our way of life depends on it.

| *Mazie Hirono*

227

The fishermen know that the sea is
dangerous and the storm terrible, but
they have never found these dangers
sufficient reason for remaining ashore.

| *Vincent van Gogh*

• *Big Island, Hawaii (USA)*

• *Varadero, Cuba*

Individuals of all ages can make an important difference in the overall health of our ocean by the actions they take every day. Simple things like picking up trash on the beach, recycling and conserving water can have a big impact on the health of our ocean.

| *Ted Danson*

The salt of those ancient seas is in our blood, its lime is in our bones. Every time we walk along a beach some ancient urge disturbs us so that we find ourselves shedding shoes and garments or scavenging among seaweed and whitened timbers like the homesick refugees of a long war.

| *Loren Eiseley*

232 • Cayo Levantado, Dominican Republic 233 left • Barbados
233 right • Dominican Republic

I had fought on behalf of man against
the sea, but I realized that it had become
more urgent to fight on behalf of the
sea against men. If man doesn't learn to
treat the oceans and the rain forest with
respect, man will become extinct.

| *Alain Bombard*

234 • Guadeloupe, France
234-235 • Pointe de la Grande Vigie, Guadalupe, France

Mankind has known hunger, cold
and violence for five hundred thousand
years. This is the first human generation
that doesn't know wholesome foods
and clean sea.

| *Francesco Burdin*

Truly, we do live on a "water planet."
For us, water is that critical issue
that we need. It's the most precious
substance on the planet, and it links
us to pretty much every environmental
issue, including climate change, that
we're facing.

| *Jacques-Yves Cousteau*

• *Fernando de Noronha, Brazil*

240-241 • *Bartolomé Island, Galápagos Islands, Ecuador* 241 top • *Galápagos fur seals* 241 bottom • *Galápagos marine iguanas*

But man, unhappily, has written one of his blackest records as a destroyer on the oceanic islands. He has seldom set foot on an island that he has not brought about disastrous changes.

| *Rachel Carson*

Coral Gardens

If everyone knew how serious this is, everyone would be activists. In our lifetime—in the last 40 years—we've lost 40% of life in the oceans.

| *Al Gore*

The tropical coral reefs have the largest biodiversity of any other environment on Earth. For example, although they amount to only 0.1% of the ocean floors, they have more than 40% of the fish species now in our seas. This fact alone would be enough to grasp their importance from a naturalistic standpoint, but if we also take the invertebrates into account and compare 10 square feet (1 square meter) of coral reef to any other environment of the same size, be it marine or terrestrial, the difference becomes so great that any other type of comparison is totally useless.

This incredible wealth of animal life has no border around it that isolates it from the rest of the sea, no passport is needed to enter or leave it, and the fish and other creatures that

normally live in the open sea or along other coastlines frequent it as "habitual tourists," so to speak, thus contributing to the overall economy of the entire marine ecosystem.

Therefore, the importance of coral reefs lies not only in their astounding beauty but also in the fact that they are a fundamental resource of the complex food chain of distant seas, which seemingly have no connection with these coral gardens.

At the very base of this entire ecosystem are the madrepores, tiny organisms with a soft body that, in colonies of billions of individuals, build with their calcareous skeletons the solid structures of coral reefs. Layer after layer can form massive heaps whose live and superficial part grows continuously over the skeletons of the dead corals underneath them, which have become wholly similar to solid rock and in certain cases may be hundreds of feet thick. A curious calculation, but one that may give us an idea of the dimensions, has shown that with the coral rock of the Great Barrier Reef in Australia, one could build 8 million pyramids as large as the Great Pyramid of Giza.

Coral thrives in the shallow water of the tropics because it needs light in order to live, not so much for themselves as for the zooxanthellae, the unicellular algae that live in the tissues of the corals in a closely knit and indissoluble symbiosis. The only part of these microalgae that we can see are the colors they impart to the corals, but in reality they constitute an enormous plant biomass. When parrotfish shatter a coral with their powerful "beaks" in order to eat its polyps, they are in fact also eating the zooxanthellae inside the latter. And these innumerable devourers of madrepores also swallow the pieces of calcareous skeletons, which, pulverized by their digestive apparatus, are expelled in the form of sand, the white sand of the marvelous tropical beaches.

Also proliferating among the corals is a large amount of encrusted algae that do not look like typical algae. Despite this, they are a favorite food for vegetarian fish such as the surgeonfish. These calcareous seaweeds also contribute directly to the construction of the reef by furnishing material that has a cementing property that consolidates the reef and makes it able to resist the powerful waves in the area facing the open sea.

Unfortunately, coral reefs are among the most endangered environments on Earth. Madrepores are extremely sensitive to pollutant agents, changes in the salinity of the water, and above all, changes in temperature. Their tolerance to global warming is minimum: the symbiosis with zooxanthellae is altered and the corals die, creating one of the saddest spectacles one can imagine—coral bleaching. This term, by now well known, indicates the process that causes coral to become totally white, leaving behind sterile stretches of calcareous structures as testimony of what had been a blaze of life and colors.

Ocean biologists have furnished data that is upsetting, to say the least: in the period from 2016 to 2017, half the coral in the Great Barrier Reef died, and coral reefs in other areas of the world suffered similar damage.

Bleaching is still taking place, with more severe phases alternating with periods of deceleration. But the overall tendency is unequivocal and extremely serious.

The rise in the sea level is also a threat for a great many islands of the coralline atolls, which often crop up just above the surface of the sea and literally risk disappearing under the rising waters.

In ideal conditions, madrepores are able to grow in order to remain always at the right sea level, following the natural effects of erosion and tectonic subsidence, but not so quickly as the most pessimistic predictions of the rise in sea level would suggest.

BARRIER REEFS

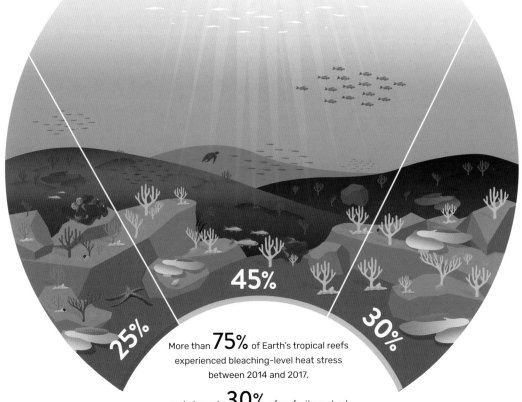

25%

45%

30%

More than **75%** of Earth's tropical reefs experienced bleaching-level heat stress between 2014 and 2017,

and at nearly **30%** of reefs, it reached mortality level.

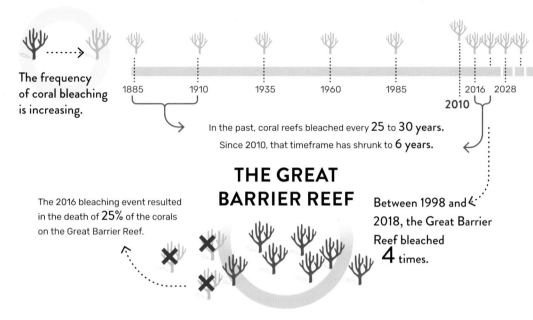

The frequency of coral bleaching is increasing.

1885 · 1910 · 1935 · 1960 · 1985 · 2010 · 2016 · 2028

In the past, coral reefs bleached every **25** to **30** years.
Since 2010, that timeframe has shrunk to **6** years.

THE GREAT BARRIER REEF

The 2016 bleaching event resulted in the death of **25%** of the corals on the Great Barrier Reef.

Between 1998 and 2018, the Great Barrier Reef bleached **4** times.

Since the Industrial Revolution, dissolved carbon dioxide is estimated to have lowered the average pH of the top layer of the oceans.

The increase in acidity is particularly bad news for shellfish and other forms of sea life that use the mineral calcium carbonate to form their shells and exoskeletons.

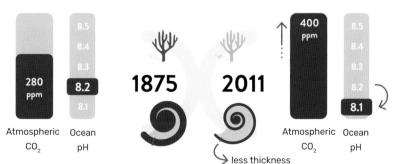

1875

2011

less thickness

280 ppm — Atmospheric CO_2

8.5 / 8.4 / 8.3 / **8.2** / 8.1 — Ocean pH

400 ppm — Atmospheric CO_2

8.5 / 8.4 / 8.3 / 8.2 / **8.1** — Ocean pH

Sources: Shape of Life, National Oceanic and Atmospheric Administration, Great Barrier Reef Marine Park Authority, Smithsonian – Find Your Blue, China Dialogue Ocean, CarbonBrief – Clear on Climate

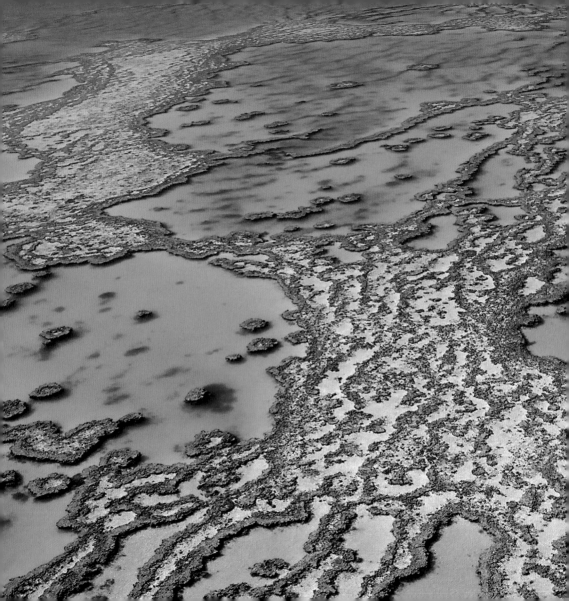

We know more about the surface of the Moon and about Mars than we do about the deep sea floor, despite the fact that we have yet to extract a gram of food, a breath of oxygen or a drop of water from those bodies.

| *Paul Snelgrove*

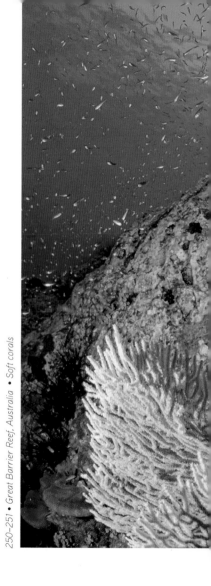

I said that the oceans were sick but they're not going to die. There is no death possible in the oceans—there will always be life—but they're getting sicker every year.

| *Jacques-Yves Cousteau*

We are being choked to death by the amount of plastic that we throw away. It's killing our oceans. It's entering into our bodies in the fish we eat.

| *Kevin Bacon*

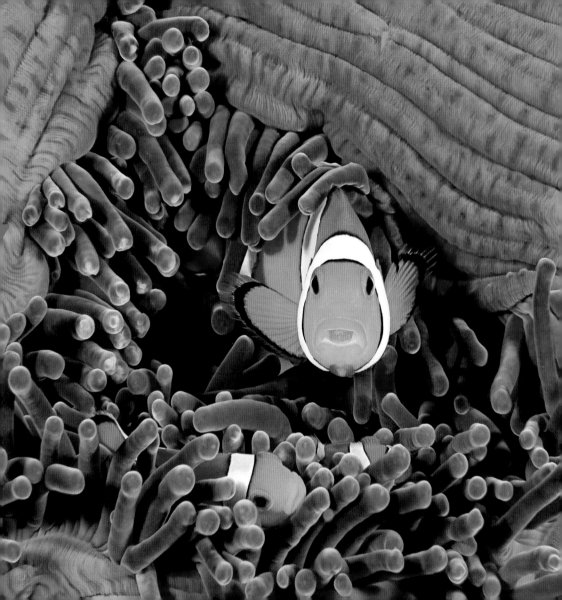

As the oceans get hotter, corals also become heat-stressed and expel the algae that live on their skeletons, resulting in coral bleaching events that can wipe out entire reefs. This destroys the habitat that supports a quarter of all marine life.

| *Barry Gardiner*

• Marbled grouper

Instead of going to the ends of the
Earth—and plumbing the depths of the
oceans—to squeeze out every last drop
of oil, we need, instead, to do everything
we can to reduce the risks of offshore
oil and gas production.

| *Frances Beinecke*

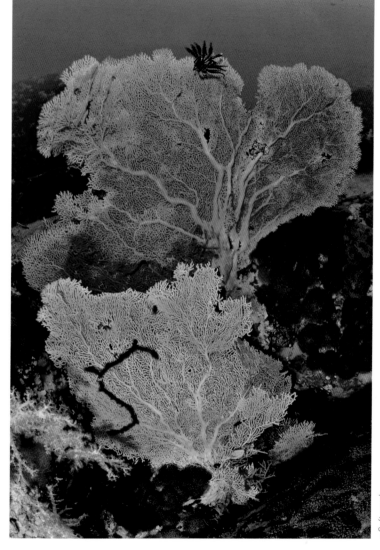

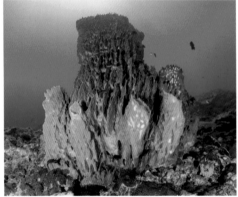

Every time you dive, you hope you'll see
something new—some new species.
Sometimes the ocean gives you a gift.

| *James Cameron*

You will love the ocean. It makes you feel so . . . I don't know. Small, but not in a bad way. Small because you realize you're part of something bigger.

| *Lauren Myracle*

Ocean acidification is often referred to as osteoporosis of the oceans because as acidity rises, shell building creatures such as lobster, oyster, crab, shrimp, and coral are unable to extract the calcium carbonate from the water that they need to build their shells and are thus unable to survive.

| *Philippe Cousteau Jr.*

The deep sea is the largest museum on Earth, it contains more history than all the museums on land combined, and yet we're only now penetrating it.

| *Robert Ballard*

Soft coral in the Philippines

Practically the whole world depends on
coral reefs, so if the coral reefs get all
killed, then the ocean will start going out
of whack, and if the ocean goes out of
whack, something might happen on land.

| *Alexander Gould*

• Dendronephthya hemprichi

From the death of coral reefs to
extinction of species, to exploitation
of natural resources, to frequent and
disastrous storms and uncontrolled
carbon emissions, catastrophe is
approaching us at an alarming pace.
Yet, we continue to live mostly oblivious
and unaware.

| *George Jacob*

• *Pink sea fan coral*

There's nothing wrong with enjoying looking at the surface of the ocean itself, except that when you finally see what goes on underwater, you realize that you've been missing the whole point of the ocean. Staying on the surface all the time is like going to the circus and staring at the outside of the tent.

| *Dave Barry*

276 • Clown triggerfish 277 top left • Titan triggerfish 277 top right • Masked butterfly fish
277 bottom left • Bluering angelfish 277 bottom right • Pufferfish

We have systematically devastated our global fisheries through destructive practices like bottom trawling . . . literally scraping up everything in their path, permanently destroying abundant underwater forests teeming with every imaginable form of wildlife. What once had looked like an endless underwater utopia is now riddled with bleached coral reefs and massive dead zones.

| *Leonardo DiCaprio*

• Green sea turtle

Don't eat shrimp—it's one of the most unsustainable fish. For every pound that's caught, 10 or 20 pounds of other stuff is killed and dumped back overboard. It's the number one killer of juvenile sea turtles in Mexico.

| *Philippe Cousteau Jr.*

• Green sea turtle and bigeye trevallies

281

The sea is emotion incarnate. It loves, hates, and weeps. It defies all attempts to capture it with words and rejects all shackles. No matter what you say about it, there is always that which you can't.

| *Christopher Paolini*

• *Southern stingrays*

• Sea fan

It's impossible to imagine our planet without coral. Think about this: if water is the blood of our planet, flowing through venous rivers, streams and into our oceans . . . What does that make coral? Our heart. We simply cannot survive without our heart, therefore it's mandatory we heal and protect our coral reefs now.

| *Ian Somerhalder*

I watched the coral reefs that I studied as a student vanish in the blink of an eye, and for decades I wrote and spoke of ocean obituaries. But big scary problems without solutions lead to apathy, not action . . . Small steps taken by many people in their backyards add up.

| *Nancy Knowlton*

286 • Honeycomb moray
286-287 • Giant moray

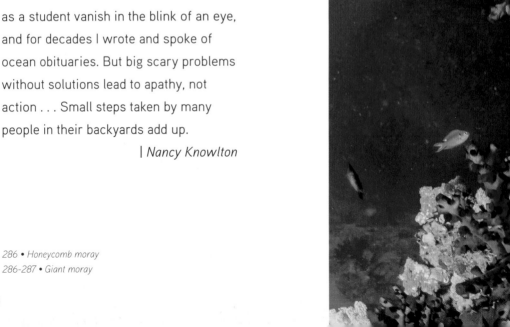

• Corals in Raja Ampat, Indonesia

Ocean acidification—the excess carbon dioxide in the atmosphere that is turning the oceans increasingly acid— is a slow but accelerating impact with consequences that will greatly overshadow all the oil spills put together.

| *Sylvia Earle*

Since 1970 one third of the world's coral reefs, the "nurseries" of the ocean, have died, and another third are expected to perish by 2030. Climate change is only adding fuel to the fire, with rapidly increasing global temperatures wreaking havoc on the delicate balance that has allowed life to flourish since the end of the last ice age.

| *Leonardo DiCaprio*

Sweetlips on a cup coral

We need a radical change in the way
we manage our oceans. Relying upon
existing frameworks is not enough.
And this is particularly the case for
areas beyond national jurisdiction which
are among the least protected areas
on our blue planet.

| *Javier Bardem*

What you see on the surface is only
a fraction of the waste that is found on
the bottom. Year after year, the situation
has worsened, and I have seen the
corals decrease or die, turning white.
With anger, I noticed how much the sea
was irreparably damaged: the fish were
decreasing, the plastic increasing. Colors
also lost their brilliance and faded.

| *Javier Goyeneche*

• *Coral formations in Togian Islands, Indonesia*

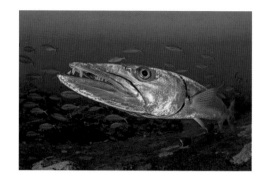

Wild fish are under threat of extinction because they're hunted to feed us. Yet land animals that we farm are under no threat of extinction. Shifting from hunting fish to farming fish could do a tremendous amount of good for wild fish.

| *Ramez Naam*

• Barracudas
298–299 • Blackspot snappers

Between the Sky
and the Sea

You cannot get through a single day without having an impact on the world around you. What you do makes a difference, and you have to decide what kind of difference you want to make.

| *Jane Goodall*

Who has not lingered at the seaside, at least once in their life, fascinated by the flight of seagulls? First they stop against the wind and remain immobile, then glide to one side and let themselves be propelled, as if connected to invisible threads that support them without any effort. Seabirds live in that borderland between two worlds and must be absolute masters of the art of flight, including knowing how not to waste energy, because when flying in the open sea so far from the coast, the slightest mistake could be fatal. Even alighting among the waves may be dangerous, and they must have enough strength to return, sooner or later, to land, maybe hundreds of miles away.

Long and narrow wings, with a wingspan of 11.5 feet (3.5 meters), much like those of a glider, allow albatrosses to make good use of the air environment, flying for incredible distances without

flapping their wings. But why travel so far, since in any case they will have to return to land in order to nest?

Seabirds' movements are determined by two closely connected necessities, food and reproduction, which lead many species to embark on long periodic migrations in order to follow the movement of the largest concentrations of their prey, which changes in the different seasons. Arctic terns are the world champions of migration. From their summer nesting zones in the Arctic regions, they head south at the end of this season, as far as the Antarctic continent, where they winter, before making the return trip: more than 43,496 miles (70,000 kilometers). This makes them the only animals that live two summers every year.

The availability of fish, which seabirds feed on, follows precise rhythms—or better, they once followed them, since now the increase in average temperatures has changed these rhythms, creating unexpected problems.

Except for the reproductive period, seabirds can leave the coasts in search of places that offer a more favorable climate and more food. But when it is time to nest, they must return to the same places in which they themselves were born. While rearing the nestlings, the parents must find as much food as possible, both for their young and themselves. Consequently, this phase must coincide with the season when the most abundance of fish is normally near those coasts.

Global warming seems to have affected the reproduction of fish accellerating it, while seabirds, less affected by this phenomenon, have not changed their breeding and rearing period. This is causing the end of the synchronization of the two phases, which in turn means a decrease in the seabirds' prey precisely when their young, which by then are somewhat grown up, need more and more food.

This is only one of the effects that global warming has had on seabirds. Some species, such as the guillemot, which nests on the Arctic sea cliffs, find it difficult to disperse heat and therefore overheat. And in fact the increase in temperature is supposed to be one of the causes of large-scale deaths registered in some recent years.

As if that were not enough, seabirds are also affected by mercury pollution in their prey, since the metal accumulates in the birds' bodies, causing serious damage to their fertility and to the growth of the chicks.

Among all the species of seabirds, the seagull may be the most opportunistic and frequents dumps in search of edible refuse, and one often sees flocks of gulls fluttering and rummaging among the piles of garbage that spill into the sea from the coastal dumping grounds.

On the other hand, some species, such as the puffin, are extremely specialized and dive into the water, coming to the surface with the characteristic "beard" of small fish it can hold in its bill. In case of a scarcity of their specific prey, these creatures risk literally dying of hunger, or at any rate, they are unable to feed their young.

The coastal differences of the Antarctic continent with respect to the Arctic seas also impinges on the seabirds' nesting method. The coasts with sheer rocky cliffs in the extreme northern regions are the ideal environment for a number of species, which often throng them with rudimentary nests or simply lay their eggs on the narrow ledges. Their eggs are very conical, so that if they are moved they merely roll in a tight circle, which prevents them from falling onto the rocks below or into the sea. At the South Pole, on the other hand, for the most part, nest-building birds prefer to flock to the subantarctic islands, competing with penguins for vast areas, and not always peacefully.

The indiscriminate hunting that seabirds still undergo despite specific laws and regulations against this practice is yet another of the many threats posed by pollution and global warming. So, the sense of freedom that the flight of seagulls transmits to us must make us reflect on what we risk losing if we do not take adequate measures.

SEABIRDS

Lord Howe Island is home to tens of thousands of seabirds. The birds that nest on the island are some of the most plastic-contaminated birds in the world. Rather than feeding their chicks the usual diet of fish, adult flesh-footed shearwaters have been providing their young with shards of plastic.

80%-90%
of all chicks studied had at least one piece of plastic in their stomach.

The normally cold California Current off the west coast of North America is one of the world's most productive ocean systems.

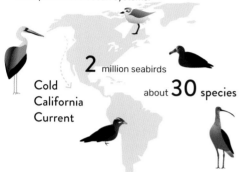

2 million seabirds

about **30** species

Cold California Current

Up and down the coast, recent **increases in sea temperature** have caused **plunging plankton density.**

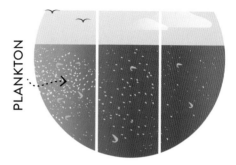

PLANKTON

Decline in numbers of **sooty shearwaters**, which formerly swarmed this vast conveyor of water.

Cold-water divers like **rhinoceros auklets** and **Cassin's auklets** appear to be withdrawing from warming Southern California waters.

2021

A 39-year study of **southern fulmar** (*Fulmarus glacialoides*) in Antarctica found that the birds forego breeding altogether during warm water anomalies, probably because **the availability of krill is so reduced.**

Sources: Journal of Animal Ecology, The National Audubon Society, Natural History Museum, London

• Blue-footed boobies, Galápagos Islands

The truth of the matter is, the birds
could very well live without us, but
many—perhaps all—of us would find life
incomplete, indeed almost intolerable
without the birds.

| *Roger Tory Peterson*

We must plant the sea and herd its animals using the sea as farmers instead of hunters. That is what civilization is all about: farming replacing hunting.

| *Jacques-Yves Cousteau*

The ocean is like a checking account where everybody withdraws but nobody makes a deposit. This is what's happening because of overfishing.

| *Enric Sala*

• *Arctic terns*

The place where there is more energy
in the world is where the water element
joins the Earth element. By the sea, in
the sun, where the fire element is also
present, the energy is even greater.
Combined with the force of the air,
given by the breeze of the wind.

| *Paracelsus*

• *Northern gannets*

When plastics do break down, they don't biodegrade; rather, they break into increasingly smaller pieces, many of which end up in the oceans as microplastics that harm aquatic life and birds.

| *David Suzuki*

• *Northern gannets*

We must recognize and respect Earth's beautiful systems of balance, between the presence of animals on land, the fish in the sea, birds in the air, mankind, water, air, and land. Most importantly there must always be awareness of the actions by people that can disturb this precious balance.

| *Margaret Mead*

• American white pelicans 322–323 • American white pelican

• Brown pelicans

Why is it that scuba divers and surfers are some of the strongest advocates of ocean conservation? Because they've spent time in and around the ocean, and they've personally seen the beauty, the fragility, and even the degradation of our planet's blue heart.

| *Sylvia Earle*

• Brown pelican

• *Brown pelican*

There are always waves on the water. Sometimes they are big, sometimes they are small, and sometimes they are almost imperceptible. The water's waves are churned up by the winds, which come and go and vary in direction and intensity, just as do the winds of stress and change in our lives, which stir up the waves in our minds.

| *Jon Kabat-Zinn*

• *Magnificent frigatebirds*

We need to start living within the planetary boundaries, focus on equity and take a few steps back for the sake of all living species. We need to protect the biosphere, the air, the oceans, the soil, the forests.

| *Greta Thunberg*

Dangerous changes in our climate, caused mainly by human activity; dead zones in our ocean, caused mainly by pollution that we create here on land; unsustainable fishing practices; unprotected marine areas, in which rare species and entire ecosystems are at risk—all those things are happening now.

| *Barack Obama*

• *Atlantic puffin*

Waves are powerful, they are connected to the sun, to the moon and to the entire human population. We must collectively make the choice to treat our oceans with respect, not tomorrow but today.

| *Jason Momoa*

We have a once-in-a-generation
chance to get things right and make
an agreement that serves the interest
of future generations. We need a
fundamental change in the way the
ocean is managed and protected.

| *Richard Branson*

• Antarctic shags

There is nothing in which the birds differ more from man than the way in which they can build and yet leave a landscape as it was before.

| *Robert Wilson Lynd*

• *Steller's sea eagles*

Seas of Ice

We ourselves feel that what we are

doing is just a drop in the ocean.

But the ocean would be less because

of that missing drop.

| *Mother Teresa*

Ice, ice as far as you can see: a white and hostile desert. This is what the polar areas of our planet look like. They appear to be similar but are really quite different, so much so that when referring to the North Pole we may also say Arctic Sea, and the South Pole is also known as the Antarctic continent.

And in fact, the ice at the North Pole does not lie on land, but is a vast floating swath, an ice pack, while Antarctica is a real continent with valleys and hills, even though it is completely covered with ice.

In the Arctic, on the other hand, in proportion to its size, the thickness of the ice pack is minimal, on average around 10 feet (3 meters), but in some points it may be several feet thicker and then

diminishes the farther it is from the North Pole, toward the northern extremities of Asia, Europe, and America. The margins of the pack break up into slabs that are more or less large, on which polar bears move about without any problem, since they can go from one slab to another by swimming in the frigid waters of the Arctic Ocean even for long distances, hence their scientific name *Ursus maritimus*. The ice areas spread in winter, up to the continental coastlines, while they contract in summer. Every year this back and forth movement of the ice allows mammals such as bears, Arctic foxes, and wolves to explore and take advantage of vaster territories.

In Antarctica the ice is much thicker and covers the continent with an ice cap whose average height is around 1 mile (1,600 meters) and in some cases more than 1.8–2.5 miles (3,000–4,000 meters). This ice desert surrounded by the ocean is the largest freshwater reserve in the world, more than 90% of the total in fact. But obviously it cannot be used, for if all the Antarctic ice melted, the sea level would rise by about 230 feet (70 meters), not to mention so many other disastrous effects this would entail. With minimum temperatures of -76°F/-94°F (-60°C/-70°C)—the record is -128.2°F (-89°C)—and winds blowing at 186 miles (300 kilometers) per hour, the Antarctic continent is beyond comparison, certainly the most inhospitable environment on Earth. Yet here too life manages to overcome the harsh conditions; indeed, the ice of Antarctica is the kingdom of emperor penguins, which return there every year to reproduce, a migration inland from the ocean that has become famous as the protagonist of so many movies and documentary films.

The coastal ice of Antarctica also follows seasonal rhythms. With lower temperatures, it spreads in the ocean with an ice pack similar to the one on the North Pole, while it contracts during the "warmer" period, when the temperature might briefly be higher than 32°F (0°C) along the coastlines located toward the lower latitudes, thus leaving stretches of the rocky coasts exposed.

It is no exaggeration to assert that despite the fact that these huge areas of ice are so inhospitable, they are a fundamental environment for all life on Earth and, sadly, are being drastically affected by the climate change that has been taking place in the last few decades. Both the northern and southern polar ice pack areas are "natural thermometers" that offer us a very evident "visual" indication of the global warming on Earth, and on a daily basis, one might say.

For example, in recent years the archipelago north of Canada, which includes the famous Northwest Passage, has become easily navigable thanks to the unprecedented decrease in superficial ice due to the melting of millions of square miles of the Arctic ice pack that has taken place since the 1980s. Furthermore, it seems that the polar ice is now melting at an even faster rate, so that the navigation routes are negotiable for longer and longer periods, much to the irresponsible satisfaction of those who navigate on them for purely commercial purposes. Naturally, the ice packs surrounding Antarctica are subject to the same fate, and in both polar zones this is causing irreversible upheavals in the marine food chains involved.

Indeed, the reduction of the ice alters the periods of greater and lesser abundance of phytoplankton, microscopic algae that in turn affect the krill that feed on it. Krill are species of pelagic crustacea that overall make up the largest animal biomass on Earth. They are so important in the marine ecosystems that they have given rise to a very meaningful saying: "Either you are krill, or you eat krill, or you eat animals that eat krill."

Unfortunately, due to changes in the environment, these crustacea are subject to progressive reduction, which is aggravated by commercial fishing. For example, in Japan alone, up to 220,400 tons (200,000 metric tons) are fished every year!

The scarcity of krill is the first step toward the decline of herring, sardines, mackerel, whales, seals, whale sharks, rays, penguins, flying seabirds, and an unimaginable quantity of marine and terrestrial species.

SEAS OF ICE

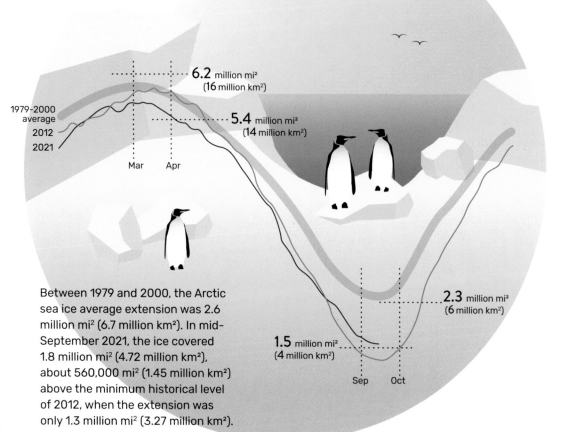

6.2 million mi²
(16 million km²)

5.4 million mi²
(14 million km²)

1979-2000
average
2012
2021

Mar   Apr

2.3 million mi²
(6 million km²)

1.5 million mi²
(4 million km²)

Sep   Oct

Between 1979 and 2000, the Arctic
sea ice average extension was 2.6
million mi² (6.7 million km²). In mid-
September 2021, the ice covered
1.8 million mi² (4.72 million km²),
about 560,000 mi² (1.45 million km²)
above the minimum historical level
of 2012, when the extension was
only 1.3 million mi² (3.27 million km²).

Arctic sea ice reaches its minimum each September. Arctic sea ice is declining at a rate of 13.1% per decade, relative to the 1981–2010 average.

In September 2021, sea ice extent stood at 1.8 million mi² (4.72 million km²), tracking above the last six years. Further south in the East Greenland Sea, there were only 45,950 mi² (119,000 km²) of sea ice, the second least amount of ice for this time of year following 2002.

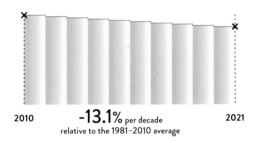

2010

-13.1% per decade
relative to the 1981–2010 average

2021

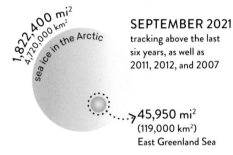

1,822,400 mi²
4,720,000 km²
sea ice in the Arctic

SEPTEMBER 2021
tracking above the last
six years, as well as
2011, 2012, and 2007

45,950 mi²
(119,000 km²)
East Greenland Sea

Antarctic sea ice usually reaches its annual maximum extent in mid- to late September, and reaches its annual minimum in late February or early March.

Over 1979–2017, Antarctic-wide sea ice extent—for the annual average, winter maximum, and summer minimum extents— showed **a slightly positive trend overall**, although some regions experienced declines.

1 million mi² (2.6 million km²)
in 2021, below the 1981–2010
climatological average, but well
above the record low recorded
in 2017.

7.3 million mi²
(19 million km²) **in 2020,**
above the 1981–2010
climatological average,
but not a record high.

Sources: NASA – Global
Climate Change,
National Snow & Ice Data
Center, National Oceanic
and Atmospheric
Administration, Istituto
Idrografico della Marina -
Italia

The Arctic is a place that historically, during all preceding human history, has largely been an icy realm with an impact on ocean currents. That, in turn, influences the temperature of the planet. The Arctic is now vulnerable because of the excess carbon dioxide in the atmosphere.

| *Sylvia Earle*

• *Northern gannets over Northern Atlantic*

• Humpback whale in Alaska 352–353 • Hubbard Glacier in Alaska

People ask: Why should I care about the ocean? Because it's the blue heart of the planet—we should take care of our heart. It's what makes life possible for us. We still have a really good chance to make things better than they are. They won't get better unless we take the action and inspire others to do the same thing. No one is without power. Everybody has the capacity to do something.

| *Sylvia Earle*

We must not sacrifice one of our remaining untamed places in reckless pursuit of oil. We know we have to leave oil in the ground, or destructive climate change will become unstoppable. If not in the pristine and vulnerable Arctic Ocean, then where?

| *Frances Beinecke*

Lofoten Islands, Norway

There was a magic about the sea.
People were drawn to it. People wanted
to love by it, swim in it, play in it, look
at it. It was a living thing that was as
unpredictable as a great stage actor:
it could be calm and welcoming, opening
its arms to embrace its audience one
moment, but then could explode with
its stormy tempers.

| *Cecelia Ahern*

Iceberg in Disko Bay, Greenland

The ocean is powerful, but not invincible. It is rich, but not inexhaustible. For humans to thrive in the coming centuries, we will have to be smarter about how we approach the 70% of our planet the ocean covers.

| *Gary E. Knell*

362-363 • Icebergs in Jökulsárlón Lagoon, Iceland   363 • Iceberg in Svalbard Islands, Norway

Tipping points are so dangerous because if you pass them, the climate is out of humanity's control: if an ice sheet disintegrates and starts to slide into the ocean there's nothing we can do about that.

| *James Hansen*

• *Humpback whales in Disko Bay, Greenland*

Ice is a supporter of life. It brings the sea animals from the north into our area and in the fall it also becomes an extension of our land. When it freezes along the shore, we go out on the ice to fish, to hunt marine mammals, and to travel. When it starts disintegrating and disappearing faster, it affects our lives dramatically.

| *Caleb Pungowiyi*

We need to save the Arctic not because
of the polar bears, and not because
it is the most beautiful place in the
world, but because our very survival
depends upon it.

| *Lewis Pugh*

By polluting the oceans, not mitigating
carbon dioxide emissions and destroying
our biodiversity, we are killing our planet.
Let us face it, there is no planet B.

| *Emmanuel Macron*

• *Walrus, Svalbard Islands, Norway*

When I was maybe eight or nine years old, I first learned about the climate crisis in school. My teachers taught me about it and we saw films and pictures of plastic in the ocean and extreme weather events. Those pictures were just stuck in my head; I thought, there is no point in anything.

| *Greta Thunberg*

• *Antarctic mountains*

Although Antarctica may seem isolated and still intact, even a remote place like this is suffering the impact of harmful human activities. For example, it is inconceivable that oil companies continue to operate there.

| *Marion Cotillard*

• *Antarctica*

Climate change is one of the greatest threats facing humanity today. Ice is trying to send us a message. Giving ice a voice was an opportunity I had to seize—before it melts away.

| *Liam Neeson*

The evidence is everywhere, from
plastic waste at the bottom of the Arctic
Ocean to flattened remains of deep
ocean reefs hundreds of miles from
land, bulldozed by bottom trawlers.
No part of the ocean, no matter how
deep or remote, is safe anymore.

| *James Cameron*

• *Humpback whale in Antarctica*

Our own greed and stupidity are taking
away the beautiful world of Arctic
Ocean sea ice, which once protected us
from the impacts of climatic extremes.
Now urgent action is needed if we are to
save ourselves from the consequences.

| *Peter Wadhams*

• *Icebergs in Antarctic Peninsula*

In this interconnected age, our problems are interconnected too. The huge amounts of plastic which find their way into our ocean do not just damage marine life, they threaten livelihoods and even find their way into our food chain too.

| *Louisa Montagu-Pollock*

• *King penguins and elephant seals, Antarctica*

Looking out at the ocean, it's easy to feel small—and to imagine all your troubles, suddenly insignificant, slipping away. Earth's seven oceans seem vast and impenetrable, but a closer look tells another story.

| *Ted Danson*

Greenhouse gases released into the atmosphere are reaching a level that will initiate dangerous effects, many of them irreversible including the extermination of countless species, melting glaciers, sea level rise and extreme regional climatic conditions, and more intense.

| *James Hansen*

• *Adélie penguins, Antarctica*

Chinstrap penguins, Antarctica

Nature is resilient if we take care to just
stop actively destroying it—it will come
back. And certainly the oceans can
come back if we take the steps that are
necessary.

| *Barack Obama*

• Antarctic fur seal

Arctic Harp seal pup populations are declining as they are commercially hunted for oil and fur and global warming causes the ice where pups are born to break up and melt. Now these sweet and adorable pups face yet another human threat: oil spills.

| *Zoe Helene*

If we look at the ocean in a calm, there is something imposing in its aspect; stretched out in its sleeping tranquility, but looking fearfully deep, and its silence seems like that of the lion when crouching for its prey.

| *Jenny M. Parker*

• *Icebergs in Andvord Bay, Antarctica*

The real cure for our environmental
problems is to understand that our job
is to salvage Mother Nature. And we are
facing a formidable challenge.

| *Jacques-Yves Cousteau*

• *Icebergs, Antarctica*

Author

VALTER FOGATO, an advertiser, graphic designer, illustrator, and author of scientific educational works, has designed and set up a large number of dioramas for various museums and visitors' centers in natural parks, including writing their explanatory panels. More specifically, he has created all the dioramas regarding world environments in Milan's Natural History Museum.

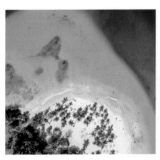